I0020026

Arduino Capacitance Meter, GPS Clock, Vehicle Tracker,Snake Game on 8x8 Matrix,Applaud Switch etc..,

ACKNOWLEDGMENTS

The writer might want to recognize the diligent work of the article group in assembling this book. He might likewise want to recognize the diligent work of the Raspberry Pi Foundation and the Arduino bunch for assembling items and networks that help to make the Internet of Things increasingly open to the overall population. Yahoo for the democratization of innovation!

INTRODUCTION

The Internet of Things (IOT) is a perplexing idea comprised of numerous PCs and numerous correspondence ways. Some IOT gadgets are associated with the Internet and some are most certainly not. Some IOT gadgets structure swarms that convey among themselves. Some are intended for a solitary reason, while some are increasingly universally useful PCs. This book is intended to demonstrate to you the IOT from the back to front. By structure IOT gadgets, the per user will comprehend the essential ideas and will almost certainly develop utilizing the rudiments to make his or her very own IOT applications. These included ventures will tell the per user the best way to assemble their very own IOT ventures and to develop the models appeared. The significance of Computer Security in IOT gadgets is additionally talked about and different systems for protecting the IOT from unapproved clients or programmers. The most significant takeaway from this book is in structure the tasks yourself.

1. CAPACITANCE METER UTILIZING ARDUINO

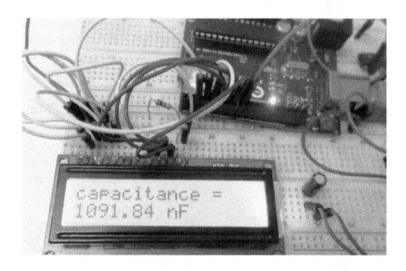

At the point when we go over circuit sheets which are recently structured or we take out one from old TV or PC, in endeavor to fix it. What's more, now and then we have to know the capacitance of specific capacitor in the board to wipe out the issue. At that point we face an issue in getting the precise estimation of capacitor from the board particularly in the event that it is a Surface Mount Device. We can purchase hardware for estimating the capacitance, yet every gadgets are expensive and not for everybody. In light of that we are gonna to structure a basic Arduino Capacitance Meter to quantify the capacitance of obscure capacitors.

This meter can be effectively made and furthermore practical. We are going to make Capacitance Meter utilizing Arduino Uno, Schmitt trigger entryway and 555 IC clock.

Required Components:

- 555 timer IC
- IC 74HC14 Schmitt trigger gate or NOT gate.
- 100nF capacitor, 1000µF capacitor
- 1K ? resistor (2 pieces), 10K? resistor
- Breadboard and some connectors.
- 16*2 LCD.

Circuit Explanation:

The circuit graph of the Capacitance Meter utilizing Arduino is appeared in underneath figure. Circuit is straightforward, a LCD is interfaced with Arduino to show the deliberate Capacitance of capacitor. A Square wave Generator Circuit (555 in Astable mode) is associated with Arduino, where we have associated the Capacitor whose capacitance should be estimated. A Schmitt trigger entryway (IC 74LS14) is utilized to guarantee that solitary rectangular wave is encouraged to Arduino. For separating the clamor we have included couple of capacitors crosswise over power.

This circuit can precisely quantify capacitances in run 10nF to 10uF.

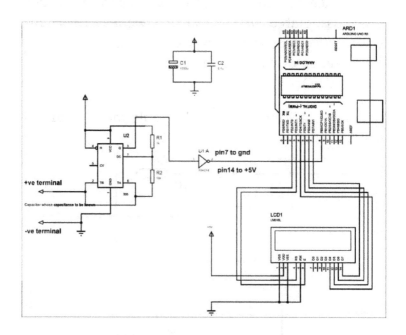

555 Timer IC Based Square Wave Generator:

Most importantly we will discuss 555 Timer IC based square wave generator, or should I say 555 Astable Multivibrator. We realize that the capacitance of a capacitor can't be estimated straightforwardly in an advanced circuit, at the end of the day the UNO manages computerized sign and it can't quantify capacitance legitimately. So we utilize 555 square wave generator circuit for connecting the capacitor to computerized world.

Essentially, the clock gives square wave yield whose recurrence straightforwardly involves to the capacitance associated with it. So first we get the square wave signal whose recurrence is the delegate of the capacitance of the obscure capacitor, and feed this sign to UNO for getting the suitable worth.

General arrangement 555 in Astable mode as an appeared in beneath figure:

The yield signal recurrence relies upon RA, RB resistors and capacitor C. The condition is given as,

Recurrence (F) = 1/(Time period) = 1.44/((RA +RB*2)*C).

Here RA and RB are opposition esteems and C is capacitance esteem. By putting the obstruction and capacitance esteems in above condition we get the recurrence of yield square wave.

We will associate 1K? as RA and 10K? as RB. So the equation becomes,

Recurrence (F) = 1/(Time period) = 1.44/(21000*C).

By revising the terms we have,

Capacitance C = 1.44/(21000*F)

In our Program Code (see underneath), for getting the capacitance esteem precisely we have determined the outcome in nF by duplicating the got outcomes (in farads) with "1000000000". Additionally we have utilized '20800' rather than 21000, on the grounds that the precise protections of RA and RB are 0.98K and 9.88K.

So in the event that we know the recurrence of the square wave we can get the capacitance esteem.

Schmitt Trigger Gate:

The sign created by the clock circuit are not totally safe to be straightforwardly given to the Arduino Uno. In light of the affectability of UNO, we use Schmitt trigger entryway. Schmitt trigger entryway is an advanced rationale door.

This door gives OUTPUT dependent on INPUT voltage level. A Schmitt Trigger has a EDGE voltage level, when the INFO sign applied to the door has a voltage level higher than the EDGE of the rationale entryway, OUTPUT goes HIGH. On the off chance that the INPUT voltage sign level is lower than THRESHOLD, the OUTPUT of door will be LOW. With that we don't normally get Schmitt trigger independently, we generally have a NOT door following the Schmitt trigger. Schmitt Trigger working is clarified here: Schmitt Trigger Gate

We are going to utilize 74HC14 chip, this chip has 6 Schmitt Trigger doors in it. These SIX entryways are associated inside as appeared in beneath figure.

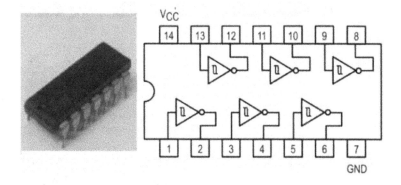

The Truth Table of Inverted Schmitt Trigger door is appear in underneath figure, with this we need to program the UNO for rearranging the positive and negative timeframes at its terminals.

$Y = \bar{A}$

Input	Output
A	Y
L	H
H	L

H = High Logic Level

L = Low Logic Level

We associate the sign created by clock circuit to ST entryway, we will have rectangular rush of rearranged timespans at the yield which is protected to be given to UNO.

Arduino measures the Capacitance:

The Uno has an extraordinary capacity pulseIn, which empowers us to decide the positive state span or negative state term of a specific rectangular wave:

```
Htime=pulseIn(8,HIGH);

Ltime = pulseIn(8, LOW);
```

The pulseIn capacity estimates the ideal opportunity for which High or Low level is available at PIN8 of Uno. The pulseIn capacity estimates this High time (Htime) and Low Time (Ltime) in smaller scale seconds. At the point when we gather Htime and Ltime into a single unit we will have the Cycle Duration, and by altering it we will have the Frequency.

When we have the recurrence, we can get the capacitance by utilizing the recipe we examined before.

Summary and Testing:

So in rundown, we interface the obscure capacitor to the 555 clock circuit, which creates a square wave yield whose recurrence is legitimately identified with capacitance of capacitor. This sign is given to UNO through ST entryway. The UNO estimates the recurrence. With recurrence known, we program the UNO to figure the capacitance by utilizing recipe examined before.

How about we see a few outcomes I got,

At the point when I associated 1uF Electrolytic Capacitor, the outcome is 1091.84 nF ~ 1uF. Furthermore, the outcome with 0.1uF Polyester Capacitor is 107.70 nF ~ 0.1uF

At that point I associated 0.1uF Ceramic Capacitor and the outcome is 100.25 nF ~ 0.1uF. Additionally the outcome with 4.7uF electrolytic capacitor is 4842.83 nF ~ 4.8uF

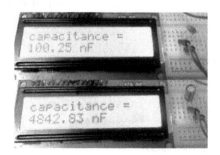

So that is the manner by which we can basically quantify the Capacitance of any capacitor.

Code

```
#include <LiquidCrystal.h>
LiquidCrystal lcd(2, 3, 4, 5, 6, 7);
int32_t Htime;
int32_t Ltime;
float Ttime;
float frequency;
float capacitance;
void setup()
{
  pinMode(8,INPUT);      //pin 8 as signal input
  lcd.begin(16, 2);
  lcd.setCursor(0,0);
  lcd.print("capacitance =");
}
void loop()
{
  for (int i=0;i<5;i++)    //measure time duration five times
  {
    Ltime=(pulseIn(8,HIGH)+Ltime)/2;    //get average for each cycle
    Htime=(pulseIn(8,LOW)+Htime)/2;
  }
  Ttime = Htime+Ltime;
  frequency=1000000/Ttime;


  capacitance  =  (1.44*1000000000)/(20800*fre-
```

```
quency);  //calculating the Capacitance in nF
  lcd.setCursor(0,1);
  lcd.print(capacitance);
  lcd.print(" nF ");
  delay(500);
}
```

2. GUI BASED HOME AUTOMATION SYSTEM UTILIZING ARDUINO AND MATLAB

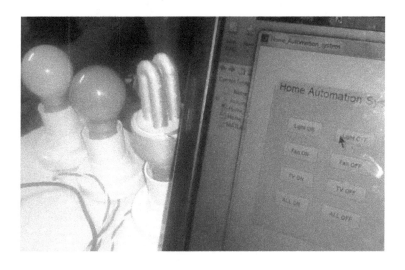

We as a whole know about the word 'Robotization', where the human collaboration is insignificant and things can be controlled consequently or remotely. Home computerization is extremely famous and requesting idea in the field of Electronics, and we are likewise attempting our earnest attempts to make this idea effectively reasonable and sensible as Electronics Projects. We have recently built up a few kinds of Home Automation Projects with a Code, if it's not too much trouble check:

- DTMF Based Home Automation

- GSM Based Home Automation utilizing Arduino

- PC Controlled Home Automation utilizing Arduino

- Bluetooth Controlled Home Automation utilizing 8051

- IR Remote Controlled Home Automation utilizing Arduino

What's more, in this task, we are gonna to fabricate our next home computerization venture utilizing MATLAB and Arduino, which is GUI Based Home Automation System Using Arduino and MATLAB

Components:

- Arduino UNO
- ULN2003
- USB Cable
- Bulb with holder
- Relay 5 volt
- Laptop
- Connecting wires

- PVT
- Power supply

Working Explanation:

Here we are utilizing MATLAB with Arduino to control the Home apparatuses, through a Graphical User Interface in Computer. Here we have utilized wired correspondence for sending information from PC (MATLAB) to Arduino. In PC side, we have utilized GUI in MATLAB to make a few catches for controlling home apparatuses. For correspondence among Arduino and MATLAB, we first need to introduce the "MATLAB and Simulink Support for Arduino" or "Arduino IO Package". To do so pursue the underneath steps:

- Download the Arduino IO Package from here. You have to Sign up before download.

- At that point Burn/transfer the adioe.pde record to the Arduino utilizing Arduino IDE. This adioe.pde document can be found in Arduino IO Package – ArduinoIO\pde\adioe \adioe.pde

- At that point open the MATLAB programming, experience the Arduino IO envelope, open the install_arduino.m document and Run it in Matlab. You will see a message of "Arduino envelopes added to the way" in direction window of MATLAB, implies MATLAB way is refreshed to Arduino organizers.

That is the means by which we cause the Arduino, to speak with MATLAB. Above technique is appropriate for "MATLAB R2013b or prior renditions", on the off chance that you are utilizing the higher variant of MATLAB (like R2015b or R2016a), you can legitimately tap on Add-ons Tab in MATLAB and afterward click "Get Hardware Support Packages", from where you can introduce Arduino bundles for MATLAB.

In the wake of introducing records, presently you can make a GUI for Home Automation Project. Essentially in GUI, we are making Push Buttons for controlling the home apparatuses from PC. Catches can be made by going into "Graphical User Interface" in "New" menu in MATLAB. Further we can set the name and shades of these catches, we have made 8 catches, in which six to ON and OFF three home machines and two catches to ON and OFF every one of the mechanical assemblies simultaneously.

Presently in the wake of making the catches, when you click on Run button in that GUI window, it will request that you spare this GUI document (with expansion .fig), otherwise called 'fig record'. As soon you spared the document, it will naturally make a code record (with expansion .m), otherwise called 'M document' (see underneath screen shot), where you can put the Code (given in Code area beneath). You can install the GUI document and Code record for this task from here: Home_Automation_system.fig and Home_Automation_system.m (right snap and select Save interface as...), or you can make them yourself like we have clarified.

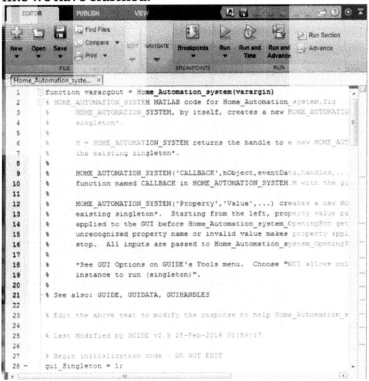

Subsequent to coding you can now at long last Run the .m record from the code window, you will see "Endeavoring association.." in the direction window. At that point an "Arduino effectively associated" message shows up, if everything goes well. Lastly you will see recently made GUI (catches) in GUI window, from where you can control the home apparatuses by simply tapping on the catches in your Computer. Ensure that Arduino is associated with Arduino by means of USB link. Here in this task we have utilized 3 bulbs for showing, which demonstrates Fan, Light and TV.

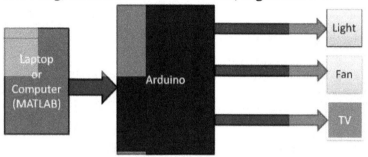

Working of the entire venture, from introducing the Arduino MATLAB bolster bundle to Turn On or OFF the apparatus, can be comprehended.

Circuit Explanation:

Circuit of this venture is exceptionally simple. Here we have utilized an Arduino UNO board and Relay Driver ULN2003 for driving transfers. Three 5 volt SPDT Relays are associated with Arduino stick number 3, 4 and 5, through transfer driver ULN2003, for controlling LIGHT, FAN and TV individually.

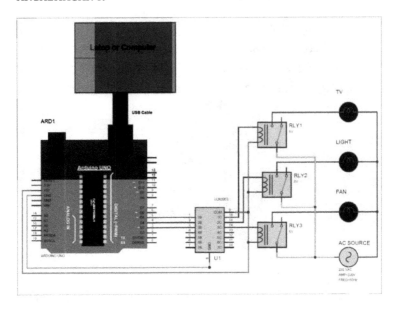

Programming Explanation:

At the point when we press any catch from the GUI window then it sends a few directions to Arduino and afterward Arduino do that activity. In the wake of introducing Arduino MATLAB IO bolster bundle, we can get to Arduino from the MATLAB by utilizing the equivalent Arduino capacities, with some little variety, as:

For making a stick HIGH in Arduino we compose code as digitalWrite(pin, HIGH)

In MATLAB we will utilize this capacity with the assistance of an item or variable like, a.digitalWrite(pin, HIGH);

furthermore, in like manner so on.

Before doing this we need to initialise variable like this:

a = Arduino('COM1');/change COM1 as indicated by your port

In this task, there is no Arduino code aside from the Arduino MATLAB bolster bundle code or record. As clarified before that code record (.m document) is naturally produced while sparing the GUI document (.fig record). There is as of now some code prewritten in .m record. Fundamentally these are Callback capacities for Push catches, implies we can characterize what ought to occur on tapping on these Push Buttons.

In MATLAB code, first we initialise sequential port and make it an article by utilizing a variable. And afterward we can begin programming like Arduino utilizing the variable.

```
clear ar;

global ar;

ar=arduino('COM13');
```

```
ar.pinMode(3, 'OUTPUT');

ar.pinMode(4, 'OUTPUT');

ar.pinMode(5, 'OUTPUT');

ar.pinMode(13, 'OUTPUT');
```

In the get back to capacity of each catch, we have composed the related code for On or OFF the separate Home Appliances, associated with Arduino by means of Relay. Like for instance, Callback work for Light ON is given underneath:

```
function light_on_Callback(hObject, eventdata, handles)

% hObject   handle to light_on (see GCBO)

% eventdata reserved - to be defined in a future version of MATLAB

% handles   structure with handles and user data (see GUIDATA)

global ar;

ar.digitalWrite(3, 1);
```

```
ar.digitalWrite(13, 1);
```

In like manner we can compose the code in the Callback elements of the considerable number of catches, to control the other associated Home Appliances, check the full MATLAB Code underneath (.m record).

Code

function varargout = Home_Automation_system(varargin)
% HOME_AUTOMATION_SYSTEM MATLAB code for Home_Automation_system.fig
%   HOME_AUTOMATION_SYSTEM, by itself, creates a new HOME_AUTOMATION_SYSTEM or raises the existing
%   singleton*.
%
%   H = HOME_AUTOMATION_SYSTEM returns the handle to a new HOME_AUTOMATION_SYSTEM or the handle to
%   the existing singleton*.
%
%
%   HOME_AUTOMATION_SYSTEM('CALLBACK',hObject,eventData,handles,...) calls the local
%   function named CALLBACK in HOME_AUTOMATION_SYSTEM.M with the given input arguments.
%
%   HOME_AUTOMATION_SYSTEM('Property','Value',...) creates a new

HOME_AUTOMATION_SYSTEM or raises the
%   existing singleton*. Starting from the left, property value pairs are
%   applied to the GUI before Home_Automation_system_OpeningFcn gets called. An
%   unrecognized property name or invalid value makes property application
%   stop. All inputs are passed to Home_Automation_system_OpeningFcn via varargin.
%
%   *See GUI Options on GUIDE's Tools menu. Choose "GUI allows only one
%   instance to run (singleton)".
%
% See also: GUIDE, GUIDATA, GUIHANDLES

% Edit the above text to modify the response to help Home_Automation_system

% Last Modified by GUIDE v2.5 28-Feb-2016 01:59:17

% Begin initialization code - DO NOT EDIT
gui_Singleton = 1;
gui_State = struct('gui_Name',   mfilename, ...
        'gui_Singleton', gui_Singleton, ...
        'gui_OpeningFcn', @Home_Automation_system_OpeningFcn, ...
        'gui_OutputFcn', @Home_Automation_system_OutputFcn, ...
        'gui_LayoutFcn', [], ...
        'gui_Callback', []);
if nargin && ischar(varargin{1})

```
  gui_State.gui_Callback = str2func(varargin{1});
end
if nargout
  [varargout{1:nargout}] = gui_mainfcn(gui_State,
varargin{:});
else
  gui_mainfcn(gui_State, varargin{:});
end
% End initialization code - DO NOT EDIT

% --- Executes just before Home_Automation_sys-
tem is made visible.
function     Home_Automation_system_OpeningFc-
n(hObject, eventdata, handles, varargin)
% This function has no output args, see OutputFcn.
% hObject   handle to figure
% eventdata  reserved - to be defined in a future ver-
sion of MATLAB
% handles   structure with handles and user data (see
GUIDATA)
% varargin          command line arguments to
Home_Automation_system (see VARARGIN)

% Choose default command line output for
Home_Automation_system
handles.output = hObject;
% Update handles structure
guidata(hObject, handles);

clear ar;
global ar;
ar=arduino('COM13');
ar.pinMode(3, 'OUTPUT');
```

```
ar.pinMode(4, 'OUTPUT');
ar.pinMode(5, 'OUTPUT');
ar.pinMode(13, 'OUTPUT');
```

% UIWAIT makes Home_Automation_system wait for user response (see UIRESUME)

% uiwait(handles.figure1);

% --- Outputs from this function are returned to the command line.

```
function varargout = Home_Automation_sys-
tem_OutputFcn(hObject, eventdata, handles)
```

% varargout cell array for returning output args (see VARARGOUT);

% hObject handle to figure

% eventdata reserved - to be defined in a future version of MATLAB

% handles structure with handles and user data (see GUIDATA)

% Get default command line output from handles structure

```
varargout{1} = handles.output;
```

% --- Executes on button press in light_on.

```
function light_on_Callback(hObject, eventdata, han-
dles)
```

% hObject handle to light_on (see GCBO)

% eventdata reserved - to be defined in a future version of MATLAB

% handles structure with handles and user data (see GUIDATA)

```
global ar;
ar.digitalWrite(3, 1);
```

```
ar.digitalWrite(13, 1);
% --- Executes on button press in light_off.
function light_off_Callback(hObject, eventdata, handles)
% hObject   handle to light_off (see GCBO)
% eventdata  reserved - to be defined in a future version of MATLAB
% handles   structure with handles and user data (see GUIDATA)
global ar;
ar.digitalWrite(3, 0);
ar.digitalWrite(13, 0);
% --- Executes on button press in fan_on.
function fan_on_Callback(hObject, eventdata, handles)
% hObject   handle to fan_on (see GCBO)
% eventdata  reserved - to be defined in a future version of MATLAB
% handles   structure with handles and user data (see GUIDATA)
global ar;
ar.digitalWrite(4, 1);
% --- Executes on button press in fan_off.
function fan_off_Callback(hObject, eventdata, handles)
% hObject   handle to fan_off (see GCBO)
% eventdata  reserved - to be defined in a future version of MATLAB
% handles   structure with handles and user data (see GUIDATA)
```

```
global ar;
ar.digitalWrite(4,0);
% --- Executes on button press in tv_on.
function tv_on_Callback(hObject, eventdata, handles)
% hObject   handle to tv_on (see GCBO)
% eventdata  reserved - to be defined in a future version of MATLAB
% handles   structure with handles and user data (see GUIDATA)
global ar;
ar.digitalWrite(5,1);
% --- Executes on button press in tv_off.
function tv_off_Callback(hObject, eventdata, handles)
% hObject   handle to tv_off (see GCBO)
% eventdata  reserved - to be defined in a future version of MATLAB
% handles   structure with handles and user data (see GUIDATA)
global ar;
ar.digitalWrite(5,0);
% --- Executes on button press in all_on.
function all_on_Callback(hObject, eventdata, handles)
% hObject   handle to all_on (see GCBO)
% eventdata  reserved - to be defined in a future version of MATLAB
% handles   structure with handles and user data (see GUIDATA)
```

```
global ar;
ar.digitalWrite(3, 1);
ar.digitalWrite(4, 1);
ar.digitalWrite(5, 1);
% --- Executes on button press in all_off.
function all_off_Callback(hObject, eventdata, handles)
% hObject   handle to all_off (see GCBO)
% eventdata  reserved - to be defined in a future version of MATLAB
% handles   structure with handles and user data (see GUIDATA)
global ar;
ar.digitalWrite(3, 0);
ar.digitalWrite(4, 0);
ar.digitalWrite(5, 0);
```

◆ ◆ ◆

3. ARDUINO GPS CLOCK

There are numerous GPS satellites around the Earth which are utilized to give the precise area of wherever. Alongside the area organizes (Latitude as well as Longitude), it likewise give other information like time, date, height, heading following edge and so forth. We have just find how to peruse this GPS information from Satellite utilizing Arduino. We are gonna to make a Global Positioning System clock utilizing the 'Time and Date' information from the Global Positioning System satellite. GPS Updated Clock is exceptionally exact and furnishes the continuous information with exactness of milliseconds.

Components:

- Arduino Uno
- 16x2 LCD
- GPS Module
- Power supply
- Connecting wires

Working Explanation:

GPS module sends the information in NMEA group, see the yield of GPS information in underneath screen capture. NMEA arrangement comprise a few sentences, wherein we need one sentence to remove the Date and Time. This sentence begins from $GPRMC and contains the directions, time and other helpful data. This $GPRMC is alluded to Recommended least explicit GPS/Transit information, and the length of this string is around 70 characters. We have recently extricated $GPGGA string in Vehicle Tracking System to discover the Latitude and Longitude Coordinates. Here is the GPS yield:

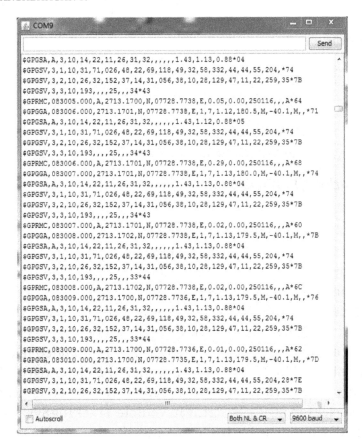

Furthermore, $GPRMC string predominantly contains speed, time, date and position

**$GPRM-
C,123519.000,A,7791.0381,N,06727.4434,E,022.
4,084.4,230394,003.1,W*6**A

$GPRMC,HHMMSS.SSS,A,latitude,N,longi-
tude,E,speed,angle,date,MV,W,CMD

Identifier	Description
RMC	Recommended Minimum sentence C
HHMMSS.SSS	Time in hour minute seconds and milliseconds format.
A	Status // A=active and V= void
Latitude	Latitude 49 deg. 16.45 min. North
N	Direction N=North, S=South
Longitude	Longitude(Coordinate)
E	Direction E= East, W=West
Speed	speed in knots
Angle	Tracking angle in degrees
Date	DATE in UTC
MV	Magnetic Variation
W	Direction of variation E/W
CMD (*6A)	Checksum Data

We can concentrate Time and Date from $GPRMC string by including the commas in the string. With the assistance of Arduino and programming, we discover $GPRMC string and stores it in a cluster, at that point Time (24 hours design) can be found after one comma and Date can be found after nine commas. Time and date are additionally spared in strings.

A GPS satellite gives Time as well as date in UTC, so we have to change over it in like manner. To change over in as indicated by Indian time, we have included 5:30 in UTC time, as Indian time is 5 and half hours in front of UTC/GMT.

Circuit Diagram:

Circuit associations of Arduino GPS Clock are straightforward. Arduino is utilized to control the entire procedure, it gets the GPS information from satellite through GPS module, extricates the Date and Time from the $GPRMC string and shows it on LCD.

Information pins D4, D5, D6, D7 of 16x2 LCD are associated with stick no. 5, 4 , 3, 2 of Arduino and order stick RS and EN of LCD are associated with stick 7 and 6 of Arduino individually. GPS collector Module Tx stick is associated with Rx stick 10 of Arduino. Ground PIN of Arduino and GPS are associated with one another. Here we have utilized SKG13BL GPS module, working at 9800 bps baud rate. Arduino is additionally arranged at 9800 bps baud rate by utilizing capacity "Serial.begin(9800)".

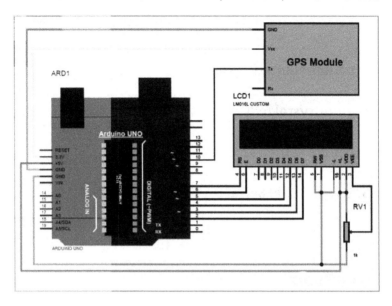

Programming Explanation:

In programming part first we incorporate libraries and characterize pins for LCD and programming sequential correspondence. Additionally characterize some factor with exhibits for putting away information. By utilizing Software Serial Library here, we have permitted sequential correspondence on stick 10 and 11, and made them Rx and Tx separately. Obviously Pin 0 and 1 of Arduino are utilized for sequential correspondence however by utilizing Software-Serial library, we can permit sequential correspondence on other computerized pins of the Arduino

```
#include<LiquidCrystal.h>

LiquidCrystal lcd(7, 6, 5, 4, 3, 2);

#include <SoftwareSerial.h>

SoftwareSerial Serial1(10, 11); // RX, TX

... ....

.... ....
```

After it we have introduced sequential correspondence and LCD in arrangement work and demonstrated an invite message on LCD.

At that point we have extricated time and date structure the got string.

```
while(x<str_lenth)

  {

  if(str[x]==',')

  comma++;
```

```
if(comma==1)

{

 x++;

 UTC_hour+=str[x++];

 ... ....

 .... ....
```

And afterward convert time and date to decimal and change it to Indian time (UTC +5:30)

```
int UTC_hourDec=UTC_hour.toInt();

int UTC_minutDec=UTC_minut.toInt();

int Second=UTC_second.toInt();

int Date=UTC_date.toInt();

int Month=UTC_month.toInt();

... ....

.... ....
```

And afterward at long last Time and Date have been appeared on LCD utilizing lcd.print work, check the full Code underneath.

Code

```
#include<LiquidCrystal.h>
LiquidCrystal lcd(7, 6, 5, 4, 3, 2);
#include <SoftwareSerial.h>
SoftwareSerial Serial1(10, 11); // RX, TX
char str[70];
char *test="$GPRMC";
int temp,i;
void setup()
{
 lcd.begin(16,2);
 Serial1.begin(9600);
 lcd.setCursor(0,0);
 lcd.print("GPS Updated Clock");
 lcd.setCursor(0,1);
 lcd.print("Hello World");
 delay(300);
}
void loop()
{
 serial1Event();
 if(temp)
 {
  lcd.clear();
  int str_lenth=i;
```

```
int x=0,comma=0;
String UTC_hour="";
String UTC_minut="";
String UTC_second="";
String UTC_date="";
String UTC_month="";
String UTC_year="";
String str1="";
while(x<str_lenth)
{
if(str[x]==',')
comma++;
 if(comma==1)
 {
  x++;
  UTC_hour+=str[x++];
  UTC_hour+=str[x++];
  UTC_minut+=str[x++];
  UTC_minut+=str[x++];
  UTC_second+=str[x++];
  UTC_second+=str[x];
  comma=2;
 }
 if(comma==10)
 {
  x++;
   UTC_date+=str[x++];
   UTC_date+=str[x++];
   UTC_month+=str[x++];
   UTC_month+=str[x++];
```

```
    UTC_year+=str[x++];
    UTC_year+=str[x];
 }
 x++;
}
int UTC_hourDec=UTC_hour.toInt();
int UTC_minutDec=UTC_minut.toInt();
int Second=UTC_second.toInt();
int Date=UTC_date.toInt();
int Month=UTC_month.toInt();
int Year=UTC_year.toInt();
int Hour=UTC_hourDec+5;
if(Hour>23)
{
 Hour-=24;
 Date+=1;
}
int Minut=UTC_minutDec+30;
if(Minut>59)
Minut-=60;



 //UTC_ind_zone_time
lcd.clear();
lcd.print("Date: ");
lcd.print(Date);
lcd.print("/");
lcd.print(Month);
```

```
lcd.print("/");
lcd.print("20");
lcd.print(Year);


  lcd.setCursor(0,1);
 lcd.print("Time: ");
 lcd.print(Hour);
lcd.print(":");
lcd.print(Minut);
lcd.print(":");
lcd.print(Second);
// delay(100);
 temp=0;
// j=0;
 i=0;
 x=0;
 str_lenth=0;
// k=0;
 }
// delay(1000);
}
void serial1Event()
{
 while(1)
 {
 while (Serial1.available())      //checking serial data
from GPS
 {
 char inChar = (char)Serial1.read();
 str[i]= inChar;          //store data from GPS into str[]
```

```
  i++;
 if(i < 7)
 {
   if(str[i-1] != test[i-1])        //checking for $GPRMC
sentence
  {
   i=0;
  }
 }
 if(i>65)
 {
 temp=1;
 break;
 }
 }
 if(temp)
 break;
 }
}
```

◆ ◆ ◆

4. INSTRUCTIONS TO USE GPS WITH ARDUINO

GPS is a valuable gadget which is utilized in numerous hardware undertakings and applications like vehicle following framework, GPS Clock, Accident Detection Alert System, traffic route and reconnaissance framework and so forth. Be that as it may, question is how to utilize the GPS and perused the information from GPS? We can without lot of a stretch get the GPS information legitimately into our PC utilizing Arduino.

Global Positioning System as well as used to identify the Latitude as well as Longitude of any area on the Earth, with precise UTC time (Universal Time Coordinated). This gadget gets the directions from the satellite for every single second, with time and date. GPS offers extraordinary precision and furthermore gives other information other than position organizes, we will into look it in the blink of an eye.

In this arduino GPS instructional exercise, we will disclose that how to Test or Interface GPS module utilizing Computer and Arduino. For interfacing Global System for Mobile with PC we either require USB to Serial Converter or Arduino Board. Here we are utilizing Arduino board to interface Global Positioning System. We just need Arduino Board, Global Positioning System module, PC and 12v/3.3v connector for power supply. Here we have utilized GPS collector Module SKG13BL (appeared in above figure).

Before interfacing it to the PC, we first need to evacuate the Arduino IC (Atmega chip) from the Arduino Board, as we just need the sequential hardware of the Arduino. This is called as the Gateway mode. Evacuating the IC is appeared in underneath figures:

Presently do the association like given in underneath picture:

- GPS TX stick to Digital PIN 1 of Arduino (TXD)

- Global Positioning System Ground Pin to GND PIN of Arduino

- Global Positioning System Power (3.3v) Pin to 3.3v PIN of Arduino

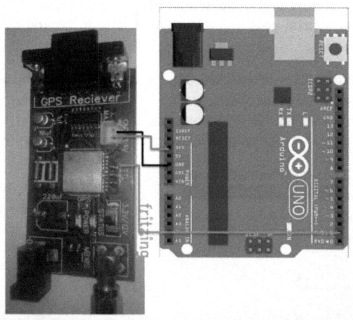

After associations, interface the USB link to the PC, open your Arduino IDE programming in PC, select com port and open sequential screen to listen the sequential port and Power up the Arduino and GPS module.

Presently you will see GPS information on Arduino Serial Monitor Window like beneath. The following are two previews, initial one is, when GPS isn't in range and second one is, when GPS in extend.

GPS Data When GPS Receiver is out of range:

GPS Data When GPS Receiver is in Range:

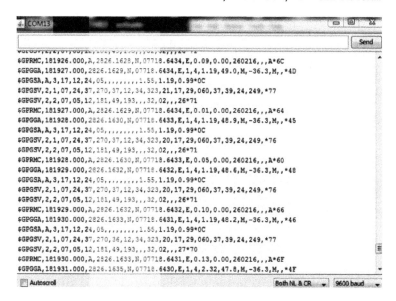

In sequential Window, you can see a few sentences that start from $ sign. These are NMEA sentences. Global Positioning System module sends the Real time following position information in NMEA design (see the screen capture above). NMEA organization comprise a few sentences, where four significant sentences are given beneath. More insight concerning the NMEA sentence and its information organization can be found here.

- $GPGGA: Global Positioning System Fix Data

- $GPGSV: GPS satellites in see

- $GPGSA: GPS DOP and dynamic satellites

- $GPRMC: Recommended least explicit GPS/ Transit information

These strings contain numerous Global Positioning System parameters like: Date,Time, Latitude, Longitude, no. of satellites in utilized, speed, elevation and numerous different things.

For any area organizes and time, we can utilize $GP-GGA and $GPRMC.

For Date and time we can utilize $GPRMC string.

At the point when we use GPS module for following any area, we just need directions and we can discover this in $GPGGA string. Just $GPGGA (Global Positioning System Fix Data) String is for the most part utilized in projects and different strings are disregarded. This string comprise fix information as beneath:

$GPG-GA,104534.000,7791.0381,N,06727.4434,E,1,08,0.9,510.4,M,43.9,M,,*47

$GPGGA,HHMMSS.SSS,latitude,N,longitude,E,FQ,NOS,HDP,altitude,M,height,M,,checksum data

Identifier	Description

$GPGGA	Global Positioning system fix data
HHMMSS.SSS	Time in hour minute seconds and milliseconds format.
Latitude	Latitude (Coordinate)
N	Direction N=North, S=South
Longitude	Longitude(Coordinate)
E	Direction E= East, W=West
FQ	Fix Quality Data
NOS	No. of Satellites being Used
HDP	Horizontal Dilution of Precision
Altitude	Altitude (meters above from sea level)
M	Meter
Height	Height
Checksum	Checksum Data

Furthermore, $GPRMC string for the most part contains speed, time, date and position

$GPRMC,123519.000,A,   7791.0381,N, 06727.4434,E,022.4,084.4,230394,003.1,W*6A

$GPRMC,HHMMSS.SSS,A,latitude,N,longitude,E,speed,angle,date,MV,W,CMD

Identifier	Description
RMC	Recommended Minimum sentence C
HHMMSS.SSS	Time in hour minute seconds and milliseconds format.
A	Status // A=active and V= void
Latitude	Latitude 49 deg. 16.45 min. North
N	Direction N=North, S=South
Longitude	Longitude(Coordinate)
E	Direction E= East, W=West
Speed	speed in knots
Angle	Tracking angle in degrees
Date	Time stamp (Date in UTC)
MV	Magnetic Variation
W	Direction of variation E/W
CMD (*6A)	Checksum Data

For the most part this string is utilized for requiring some investment, date and speed.

5. ARDUINO BASED VEHICLE TRACKER UTILIZING GPS AND GSM

In our past article, we have found out about "How to interface Global Positioning System module with Computer as well as How to make a GPS refreshed Clock". In this undertaking we are proceeding step ahead with GPS and going to follow a vehicle utilizing GPS and GSM. This Vehicle Tracking System can likewise be utilized for Accident Detection Alert System, Soldier Tracking System as well as some more, by simply rolling out scarcely any improvements in equipment and programming.

Following of vehicle is a procedure where we track the vehicle area in type of Latitude and Longitude (GPS arranges). GPS Coordinates are the estimation of an area. This framework is proficient for open air application reason.

This sort of Vehicle Tracking System Project is broadly in following Cabs/Taxis, taken vehicles, school/universities transports and so on.

Components Required:

- Arduino
- GPS Module
- GSM Module
- Power Supply
- 16x2 LCD
- 10 K POT
- Connecting Wires

GPS Module and Its Working:

GPS represents Global Positioning System and used to recognize the Latitude and Longitude of any area on the Earth, with careful UTC time (Universal Time Coordinated). GPS module is the principle segment in our vehicle following framework venture. This gadget gets the directions from the satellite for every single second, with time and date.

GPS module sends the information identified with following situation continuously, and it sends such a large number of information in NMEA position (see the screen capture beneath). NMEA organization comprise a few sentences, where we just need one sentence. This sentence begins from $GPGGA and contains the directions, time and other helpful data. This GPGGA is alluded to Global Positioning System Fix Data. Find out about Reading GPS information and its strings here.

We can concentrate facilitate from $GPGGA string by including the commas in the string. Assume you discover $GPGGA string and stores it in an exhibit, at that point Latitude can be found after two commas and Longitude can be found after four commas.

Presently these scope and longitude can be placed in different exhibits.

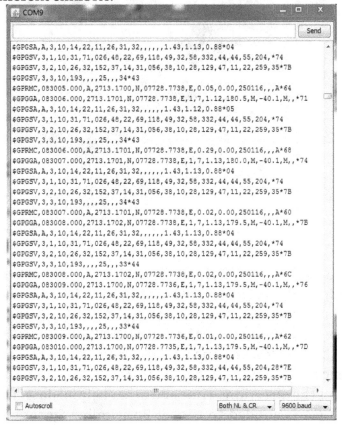

The following is the $GPGGA String, alongside its depiction:

$GPG-
GA,104534.000,7791.0381,N,06727.4434,E,1,08,0.
9,510.4,M,43.9,M,,*47

$GPGGA,HHMMSS.SSS,latitude,N,longitude,E,FQ,NOS,HDP,altitude,M,height,M,,checksum information

Identifier	Description
$GPGGA	Global Positioning system fix data
HHMMSS.SSS	Time in hour minute seconds and milliseconds format.
Latitude	Latitude (Coordinate)
N	Direction N=North, S=South
Longitude	Longitude(Coordinate)
E	Direction E= East, W=West
FQ	Fix Quality Data
NOS	No. of Satellites being Used
HPD	Horizontal Dilution of Precision
Altitude	Altitude from sea level
M	Meter
Height	Height
Checksum	Checksum Data

Circuit Explanation:

Circuit Connections of this Vehicle Tracking System Project is basic. Here Tx stick of GPS module is straightforwardly associated with advanced stick number 10 of Arduino. By utilizing Software Serial Library here, we have permitted sequential correspondence on stick 10 and 11, and made them Rx and Tx separately and left the Rx stick of GPS Module open. Obviously Pin 0 and 1 of Arduino are utilized for sequential correspondence however by utilizing SoftwareSerial library, we can permit sequential correspondence on other computerized pins of the Arduino. 12 Volt supply is utilized to control the GPS Module.

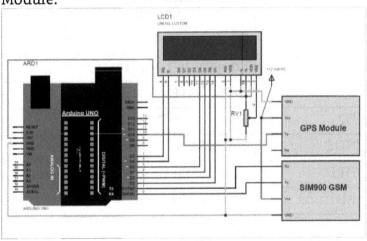

GSM module's Tx and Rx pins of are legitimately associated with stick Rx and Tx of Arduino. GSM module is additionally controlled by 12v stockpile. A discretionary LCD's information pins D4, D5, D6 as well as D7 are associated with stick number 5, 4, 3, and 2 of Arduino. Order stick RS and EN of LCD are associated with stick number 2 and 3 of Arduino and RW stick is straightforwardly associated with ground. A Potentiometer is additionally utilized for setting complexity or brilliance of LCD.

Working Explanation:

In this venture, Arduino is used for controlling entire the procedure with a Global Positioning System Receiver as well as Global System for Mobile module. Global Positioning System Receiver is used for identifying directions of the vehicle, Global System for Mobile module is used for sending the directions to client by SMS. What's more, a discretionary 16x2 LCD is likewise utilized for showing status messages or facilitates. We have utilized Global Positioning System Module SKG13BL and Global System for Mobile Module SIM900A.

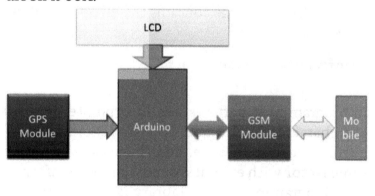

Right at the moment when we prepared with our equipment subsequent to programming, we can introduce it in our vehicle and power it up. At that point we simply need to send a SMS, "Track Vehicle", to the framework that is set in our vehicle. We can likewise utilize some prefix (#) or addition (*) like #Track Vehicle*, to appropriately distinguish the beginning and closure of the string, as we did in these undertakings: GSM Based Home Automation and Wireless Notice Board

Sent message is gotten by GSM module which is associated with the framework and sends message information to Arduino. Arduino understands it and concentrate principle message from the entire message. And afterward contrast it and predefined message in Arduino. In case any match happens, at that point Arduino peruses facilitates by separating $GPGGA String from GPS module information (GPS working clarified above) and send it to client by utilizing GSM module. This message contains the directions of vehicle area.

Programming Explanation:

In programming part first we incorporate libraries and characterize pins for LCD and programming sequential correspondence. Additionally characterize some factor with exhibits for putting away information. Programming Serial Library is utilized to permit sequential correspondence on stick 10 and 11.

```
#include<LiquidCrystal.h>
```

```
LiquidCrystal lcd(7, 6, 5, 4, 3, 2);

#include <SoftwareSerial.h>

SoftwareSerial gps(10,11); // RX, TX

char str[70];

String gpsString="";

... ....

.... ....
```

Here cluster str[70] is utilized for putting away got message from GSM module and gpsString is utilized for putting away GPS string. burn *test="$GPGGA" is utilized to look at the correct string that we requirement for facilitates.

After it we have introduced sequential correspondence, LCD, GSM and GPS module in arrangement work and demonstrated an invite message on LCD.

```
void setup()

{

lcd.begin(16,2);
```

```
Serial.begin(9600);

gps.begin(9600);

lcd.print("Vehicle Tracking");

lcd.setCursor(0,1);

... ....

.... ....
```

In circle work we get message and GPS string.

```
void loop()

{

  serialEvent();

  if(temp)

  {

    get_gps();

    tracking();

  }
```

```
}
```

Capacities void init_sms and void send_sms() are accustomed to initialising and sending message. Utilize legitimate 10 digit Cell telephone no, in init_sms work.

Capacity void get_gps() has been used to extricate the directions from the got string.

Capacity void gpsEvent() is utilized for getting GPS information into the Arduino.

Capacity void serialEvent() is utilized for getting message from GSM and contrasting the got message and predefined message (Track Vehicle).

```
void serialEvent()

{

  while(Serial.available())

  {

   if(Serial.find("Track Vehicle"))

   {

    temp=1;
```

```
   break;

 }

 ... ....

 .... ...
```

Introduction work 'gsm_init()' is utilized for initialising and designing the GSM Module, where right off the bat, GSM module is checked whether it is associated or not by sending 'AT' direction to GSM module. In case reaction OK is gotten, implies it is prepared. Framework continues checking for the module until it gets prepared or until 'alright' is gotten. At that point ECHO is killed by sending the ATE0 direction, generally GSM module will resound every one of the directions. At that point at long last Network accessibility is checked through the 'AT+CPIN?' order, whenever embedded card is SIM card and PIN is available, it gives the reaction +CPIN: READY. This is likewise check over and again until the system is found.

Check all the above capacities in Code Section underneath.

Code

```
#include<LiquidCrystal.h>
LiquidCrystal lcd(7, 6, 5, 4, 3, 2);
#include <SoftwareSerial.h>
```

```
SoftwareSerial gps(10,11); // RX, TX
//String str="";
char str[70];
String gpsString="";
char *test="$GPGGA";
String latitude="No Range   ";
String longitude="No Range   ";
int temp=0,i;
boolean gps_status=0;
void setup()
{
 lcd.begin(16,2);
 Serial.begin(9600);
 gps.begin(9600);
 lcd.print("Vehicle Tracking");
 lcd.setCursor(0,1);
 lcd.print("  System  ");
 delay(2000);
 gsm_init();
 lcd.clear();
 Serial.println("AT+CNMI=2,2,0,0,0");
 lcd.print("GPS Initializing");
 lcd.setCursor(0,1);
 lcd.print(" No GPS Range ");
 get_gps();
 delay(2000);
 lcd.clear();
 lcd.print("GPS Range Found");
 lcd.setCursor(0,1);
 lcd.print("GPS is Ready");
```

```
 delay(2000);
 lcd.clear();
 lcd.print("System Ready");
 temp=0;
}
void loop()
{
 serialEvent();
 if(temp)
 {
  get_gps();
  tracking();
 }
}
void serialEvent()
{
 while(Serial.available())
 {
  if(Serial.find("Track Vehicle"))
  {
   temp=1;
   break;
  }
  else
  temp=0;
 }
}
void gpsEvent()
{
 gpsString="";
```

```
while(1)
{
  while (gps.available()>0)        //checking serial data
from GPS
  {
  char inChar = (char)gps.read();
    gpsString+= inChar;            //store data from GPS
into gpsString
  i++;
  if(i < 7)
  {
    if(gpsString[i-1] != test[i-1])    //checking for $GP-
GGA sentence
    {
      i=0;
      gpsString="";
    }
  }
  if(inChar=='\r')
  {
  if(i>65)
  {
   gps_status=1;
   break;
  }
  else
  {
   i=0;
  }
  }
```

```
  }
  if(gps_status)
  break;
  }
}
void gsm_init()
{
 lcd.clear();
 lcd.print("Finding Module..");
 boolean at_flag=1;
 while(at_flag)
 {
  Serial.println("AT");
  while(Serial.available()>0)
  {
   if(Serial.find("OK"))
   at_flag=0;
  }


    delay(1000);
 }
 lcd.clear();
 lcd.print("Module Connected..");
 delay(1000);
 lcd.clear();
 lcd.print("Disabling ECHO");
 boolean echo_flag=1;
 while(echo_flag)
 {
```

```
Serial.println("ATE0");
while(Serial.available()>0)
{
 if(Serial.find("OK"))
 echo_flag=0;
}
 delay(1000);
}
lcd.clear();
lcd.print("Echo OFF");
delay(1000);
lcd.clear();
lcd.print("Finding Network..");
boolean net_flag=1;
while(net_flag)
{
 Serial.println("AT+CPIN?");
 while(Serial.available()>0)
 {
  if(Serial.find("+CPIN: READY"))
  net_flag=0;
 }
 delay(1000);
}
lcd.clear();
lcd.print("Network Found..");
 delay(1000);
lcd.clear();
}
void get_gps()
```

```
{
 gps_status=0;
 int x=0;
 while(gps_status==0)
 {
 gpsEvent();
 int str_lenth=i;
 latitude="";
 longitude="";
 int comma=0;
 while(x<str_lenth)
 {
  if(gpsString[x]==',')
  comma++;
  if(comma==2)    //extract latitude from string
  latitude+=gpsString[x+1];
    else if(comma==4)      //extract longitude from
string
  longitude+=gpsString[x+1];
  x++;
 }
 int l1=latitude.length();
 latitude[l1-1]='';
 l1=longitude.length();
 longitude[l1-1]='';
 lcd.clear();
 lcd.print("Lat:");
 lcd.print(latitude);
 lcd.setCursor(0,1);
 lcd.print("Long:");
```

```
 lcd.print(longitude);
 i=0;x=0;
 str_lenth=0;
 delay(2000);
 }
}
void init_sms()
{
 Serial.println("AT+CMGF=1");
 delay(400);
  Serial.println("AT+CMGS=\"+91*********\"");    // use
your 10 digit cell no. here
 delay(400);
}
void send_data(String message)
{
 Serial.println(message);
 delay(200);
}
void send_sms()
{
 Serial.write(26);
}
void lcd_status()
{
 lcd.clear();
 lcd.print("Message Sent");
 delay(2000);
 lcd.clear();
 lcd.print("System Ready");
```

```
 return;
}
void tracking()
{
  init_sms();
  send_data("Vehicle Tracking Alert:");
  send_data("Your Vehicle Current Location is:");
  Serial.print("Latitude:");
  send_data(latitude);
  Serial.print("Longitude:");
  send_data(longitude);
  send_data("Please take some action soon..\nThank-
you");
  send_sms();
  delay(2000);
  lcd_status();
}
```

◆ ◆ ◆

6. SNAKE GAME ON 8X8 MATRIX UTILIZING ARDUINO

Snake Game has been prevalent since the start of the Mobile telephones. At first it was come in Black and white mobile phones, and before long turned out to be well known. At that point with the progression of the Cellphones, this game has additionally changed a great deal, and now numerous graphical and vivid forms of this game are accessible.

Snake game has likewise become exceptionally prominent DIY venture for hardware Hobbyist and Students. So today we will illustrate, Arduino Snake Game, with all its fundamental functionalities, while keeping it basic simultaneously.

Components Used:

- Arduino UNO
- Shift Register 74HC595
- 8x8 LED Dot Matrix Display
- POT 1K
- 16x2 LCD
- Connecting wires
- Push Buttons
- Power Supply
- Bread Board

Working Explanation:

This is minimal entangled game to fabricate. However, in this instructional exercise, we have made it basic for you. To make this venture, we have utilized a 8x8 red shading Dot lattice show for showing the snake and its nourishment speck, a LCD for showing the focuses or score, 5 push catches for giving bearings and start the game lastly an Arduino UNO for controlling the entire the procedure. Stick outline of 8x8 LED Dot Matrix Display with its unique picture has been given underneath:

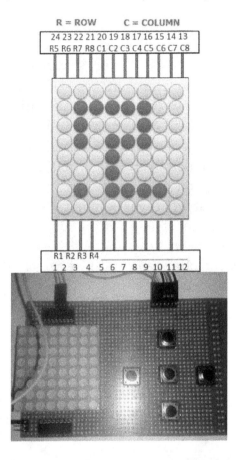

At the point when we catalyst the circuit, first we show an invite message and afterward a "Press Start To Play" indication on the LCD. After this, LCD shows the score as zero and dab framework show shows two specks as snake and a solitary spot as nourishment.

Presently client need to press the center catch to begin the game and snake start moving upward way of course. At that point client needs to provide guidance to wind by squeezing the 'Bearing keys' around the center catch. Here we have utilized five keys (push catches) to be specific Left key, Right key, Up key, Down key and Start key. At whatever point the snake scopes to the nourishment spot or eats the nourishment, score increments by 5 each time and the Snake length is expanded by one dab (LED) each time, likewise snake speed become quicker than previously. What's more, at whatever point snake would strike at any divider or reach toward the finish of LED framework, at that point it would end the ("Game Over"). At that point client needs to begin game again by squeezing start key.

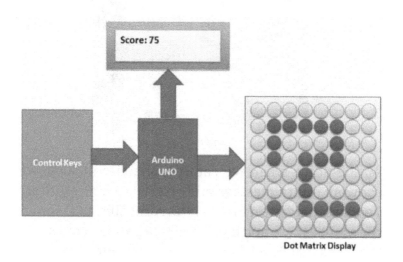

Dot Matrix Display

Circuit Explanation:

Circuit of this Snake Game Project is minimal complex. Here we have associated speck grid show by utilizing Shift Register 74HC595. Here two move registers are utilized, one for driving the segments as well as second for driving the columns. Control pins of both the registers, Column move register and line move register (SH, ST), are legitimately associated with Arduino's stick number 14 and 16 individually. Also, DS stick of section move register and column move register are straightforwardly associated with stick number 15 and 17 of Arduino. Start button for start the game is associated at stick number 3, left bearing catch at stick 4, right course button at stick 6, up heading button at bind 2 and course button at stick 5. A LCD is likewise associated in our equipment to show score. RS and EN pins are legitimately associated at stick 13 and 12. RW stick is legitimately ground. Also, information pins d4-d7 are associated at stick 11, 10, 9, 8 of Arduino. Rest of association are appeared in the circuit outline.

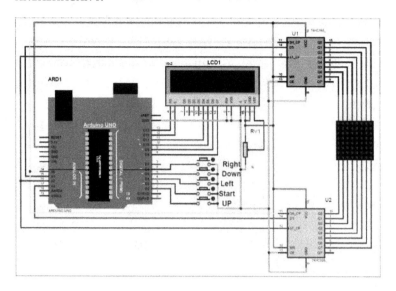

Programming Explanation:

To compose this Arduino snake game code, most importantly we incorporate header documents and characterize pins for LCD. And afterward characterize a few pins for bearing catches and information stick for move registers.

```
#include<LiquidCrystal.h>

LiquidCrystal lcd(13,12,11,10,9,8);

#define ds_col 15

#define sh_col 16
```

```
#define st_col 14

#define ds_row 17

#define start 3

#define up 2

#define down 5

#define left 4

#define right 6
```

At that point we instate some of things that we have utilized in the program. In the arrangement work we introduce LCD, provide guidance to information yield pins, pull-up the bits and demonstrating welcome message on LCD.

```
void setup()

{

  lcd.begin(16,2);

  pinMode(ds_col, OUTPUT);

  pinMode(sh_col, OUTPUT);
```

```
pinMode(st_col, OUTPUT);

pinMode(ds_row, OUTPUT);

pinMode(start, INPUT);

... ....

.... ....
```

And afterward we start game in circle work.

```
void show_snake(int temp)

{

for(int n=0;n<temp;n++)

{

 int r,c;

 for(int k=0;k<21;k++)

 {

 ... ....

 .... ....
```

Here we have utilized the underneath work for perusing input course from the push button.

```
void read_button()

{

if(!digitalRead(left))

{

  move_r=0;

  move_c!=-1 ? move_c=-1 : move_c=1;

  while(!digitalRead(left));

  ... .....

  .... ....
```

Check the full C Code of Snake Game underneath.

Code

```
#include<LiquidCrystal.h>
LiquidCrystal lcd(13,12,11,10,9,8);
#define ds_col 15
#define sh_col 16
```

```
#define st_col 14
#define ds_row 17
#define start 3
#define up 2
#define down 5
#define left 4
#define right 6
char Col[21],Row[21],move_c,move_r;
int colum_data(int temp)
{
 switch(temp)
 {
  case 1: return 1;break;
  case 2: return 2; break;
  case 3: return 4; break;
  case 4: return 8; break;
  case 5: return 16; break;
  case 6: return 32; break;
  case 7: return 64; break;
  case 8: return 128; break;
  default: return 0; break;
 }
}
int row_data(int temp)
{
 switch(temp)
 {
  case 1: return 1;break;
  case 2: return 2; break;
  case 3: return 4; break;
```

```
 case 4: return 8; break;
 case 5: return 16; break;
 case 6: return 32; break;
 case 7: return 64; break;
 case 8: return 128; break;
 default: return 0; break;
 }
}
void read_button()
{
if(!digitalRead(left))
{
 move_r=0;
 move_c!=-1 ? move_c=-1 : move_c=1;
 while(!digitalRead(left));
}
if(!digitalRead(right))
{
 move_r=0;
 move_c!=1 ? move_c=1 : move_c=-1;
 while(!digitalRead(right));
}
if(!digitalRead(up))
{
 move_c=0;
 move_r!=-1 ? move_r=-1 : move_r=1;
 while(!digitalRead(up));
}
if(!digitalRead(down))
{
```

```
  move_c=0;
  move_r!=1 ? move_r=1 : move_r=-1;
  while(!digitalRead(down));
 }
}
void show_snake(int temp)
{
for(int n=0;n<temp;n++)
{
 int r,c;
 for(int k=0;k<21;k++)
 {
 int temp1=Col[k];
 c=colum_data(temp1);
 int temp2=Row[k];
 r=0xff-row_data(temp2);
 for(int i=0;i<8;i++)
 {
    int ds=(c & 0x01);
    digitalWrite(ds_col, ds);
    ds=(r & 0x01);
    digitalWrite(ds_row, ds);
    digitalWrite(sh_col, HIGH);
    c>>=1;
    r>>=1;
    digitalWrite(sh_col, LOW);
 }
 digitalWrite(st_col, HIGH);
 digitalWrite(st_col, LOW);
 read_button();
```

```
  delayMicroseconds(500);
 }
 }
}
void setup()
{
  lcd.begin(16,2);
  pinMode(ds_col, OUTPUT);
  pinMode(sh_col, OUTPUT);
  pinMode(st_col, OUTPUT);
  pinMode(ds_row, OUTPUT);
  pinMode(start, INPUT);
  pinMode(up, INPUT);
  pinMode(down, INPUT);
  pinMode(left, INPUT);
  pinMode(right, INPUT);
  digitalWrite(up, HIGH);
  digitalWrite(down, HIGH);
  digitalWrite(left, HIGH);
  digitalWrite(right, HIGH);
  digitalWrite(start, HIGH);
  lcd.setCursor(0,0);
  lcd.print(" Snake game  ");
  lcd.setCursor(0,1);
  lcd.print("Hello World");
  delay(2000);
  lcd.setCursor(0,0);
  lcd.print(" Press Start ");
  lcd.setCursor(0,1);
  lcd.print("   To Play   ");
```

```
  delay(2000);
}
void loop()
{
 int j,k,Speed=40,score=0;
 j=k=move_c=0;
 move_r=1;
 lcd.clear();
 lcd.setCursor(0,0);
 lcd.print("Score: ");
 lcd.print(score);
 while(1)
 {
 for(int i=3;i<21;i++)
 {
  Row[i]=100;
  Col[i]=100;
 }
 Row[0]=rand()%8+1;
 Col[0]=rand()%8+1;
 Row[1]=1;
 Col[1]=1;
 Row[2]=2;
 Col[2]=1;
 j=2,k=1;
 while(k==1)
 {
 move_c=0;
 move_r=1;
 show_snake(1);
```

```
lcd.setCursor(7,0);
lcd.print(score);
if(!digitalRead(start))
{
 k=2;
 Speed=40;
 score=0;
}
}


 while(k==2)
{
   show_snake(Speed);
   if(Row[1]>8 || Col[1]>8 || Row[1]<0 || Col[1]<0)
   {
   Row[1]=1;
   Col[1]=1;
   k=1;
   lcd.setCursor(0,1);
   lcd.print("Game Over");
   delay(5000);
   score=0;
   lcd.clear();
   lcd.setCursor(0,0);
   lcd.print("Score: ");
   lcd.print(score);
   }
                if(Row[0]==Row[1]+move_r     &&
Col[0]==Col[1]+move_c)
   {
```

```
    j++;
    Speed-=2;
    score=score+5;
    lcd.setCursor(7,0);
    lcd.print(score);
    Row[0]=rand()%8+1;
    Col[0]=rand()%8+1;
}
for(int i=j;i>1;i--)
{
 Col[i]=Col[i-1];
 Row[i]=Row[i-1];
}
Col[1]=Col[2]+move_c;
Row[1]=Row[2]+move_r;
}
}
}
```

7. GLOBAL SYSTEM FOR MOBILE BASED HOME AUTOMATION UTILIZING ARDUINO

Cell phone is a progressive development of the century. It was fundamentally intended for making and accepting calls and instant messages, yet it has gotten the entire world after the Smart telephone comes into the image. In this undertaking we are building a home robotization framework, where one can control the home machines, utilizing the straightforward GSM based telephone, just by sending SMS through his telephone. In this undertaking, no Smart telephone is required, only the old GSM telephone will work to turn ON and OFF any home electronic apparatuses, from anyplace. You can likewise check some increasingly Wireless Home Automation extends here: IR Remote Controlled Home Automation utilizing Arduino, Bluetooth Controlled Home Automation alongside DTMF Based Home Automation, PC Controlled Home Automation utilizing Arduino.

Working Explanation

In this venture, Arduino is used for controlling entire the procedure. Here we have utilized GSM remote correspondence for controlling home machines. We send a few directions like "#A.light on*", "#A.light off*, etc for controlling AC home machines. Subsequent to getting given directions by Arduino through GSM, Arduino send sign to transfers, to turn ON or OFF the home apparatuses utilizing a hand-off driver.

Circuit Components:

- Arduino UNO
- ULN2003
- GSM Module
- Bulb with holder
- Relay 5 volt

- Bread board
- Connecting wires
- Power supply
- 16x2 LCD
- Cell phone

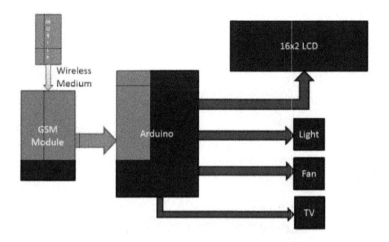

Here we have utilized a prefix in direction string that is "#A.". This prefix is utilized to distinguish that the principle direction is coming beside it and * toward the finish of string demonstrates that message has been finished.

At the point when we send SMS to Global System for Mobile module by Mobile, at that point GSM gets that SMS as well as sends it to Arduino. Presently Arduino peruses this SMS and concentrate principle direction from the got string and stores in a variable. After this, Arduino contrast this string and predefined string. In the event that match happened, at that point Arduino sends sign to hand-off by means of transfer driver for killing ON and the home apparatuses. What's more, relative outcome likewise prints on 16x2 LCD by utilizing fitting directions.

Here in this undertaking we have utilized 3 zero watt bulb for exhibition which demonstrates Fan, Light and TV.

The following is the rundown of messages which we send through SMS, to kill On and the Fan, Light and TV:

S.no.	Message	Operation
1	#A.fan on*	Fan ON
2	#A.fan off*	Fan OFF
3	#A.light on*	Light ON
4	#A.light off*	Light OFF
5	#A.tv on*	TV ON
6	#A.tv off*	TV Off
7	#A.all on*	All ON
8	#A.all off*	All OFF

GSM Module:

GSM module is utilized in numerous specialized gadgets which depend on Global System for Mobile

Communications innovation. It is utilized to collaborate with GSM system utilizing a PC. GSM module just comprehends AT directions, and can react likewise. The most essential order is "AT", on the off chance that GSM react OK, at that point it is working great else it react with "Mistake". There are different AT directions like ATA for answer a call, ATD to dial a call, AT+CMGR to peruse the message, AT+CMGS to send the sms and so forth. AT directions ought to be trailed via Carriage return for example \r (0D in hex), like "AT+CMGS\r". We can utilize GSM module utilizing these directions:

ATE0 - For reverberation off

AT+CNMI=2,2,0,0,0 <ENTER> - Auto opened message Receiving. (No compelling reason to open message)

ATD<Mobile Number>; <ENTER> - making a call (ATD +919610126059;\r\n)

AT+CMGF=1 <ENTER> - Selecting Text mode

AT+CMGS="Mobile Number" <ENTER> - Assigning beneficiary's versatile number

>>Now we can compose our message

>>After composing message

Ctrl+Z send message direction (26 in decimal).

ENTER=0x0d in HEX

The SIM900 is a finished Quad-band Global System for Mobile/General Packet Radio Service Module which conveys GSM/GPRS 850/900/1800/1900MHz execution for voice, SMS as well as Data with low power utilization.

Circuit Description

Associations of this GSM based home robotization circuit are very straightforward, here a fluid precious stone showcase is utilized for showing status of home apparatuses which is legitimately associated with arduino in 4-piece mode. Information pins of LCD to be specific RS, EN, D4, D5, D6, D7 are associated with arduino advanced stick number 6, 7, 8, 9, 10, 11. Furthermore, Rx and Tx stick of GSM module is straightforwardly associated at Tx as well as Rx stick of Arduino separately. Furthermore, GSM module is controlled by utilizing a 12 volt connector. 5 volt SPDT 3 transfers are utilized for controlling LIGHT, FAN and TV. What's more, transfers are associated with arduino stick number 3, 4 and 5 through hand-off driver ULN2003 for controlling LIGHT, FAN and TV individually.

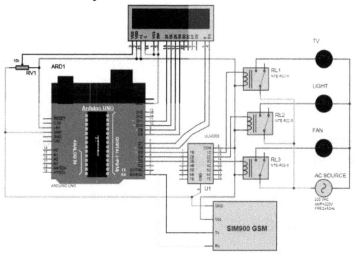

Code Description

In programming some portion of this undertaking, as a matter of first importance in programming we incorporates library for fluid precious stone showcase and afterward we characterizes information and control pins for LCD and home machines.

```
#include<LiquidCrystal.h>
```

```
LiquidCrystal lcd(6,7,8,9,10,11);

#define Fan 3

#define Light 4

#define TV 5

int temp=0,i=0;

int led=13;
```

After this sequential correspondence is introduced at 9600 bps and provides guidance to utilized stick.

```
void setup()

{

  lcd.begin(16,2);

  Serial.begin(9600);

  pinMode(led, OUTPUT);

  pinMode(Fan, OUTPUT);

   pinMode(Light, OUTPUT);
```

```
pinMode(TV, OUTPUT);
```

For accepting information sequentially we have utilized two capacities one is Serial.available which checks whether any sequential information is coming and other one is Serial.read which peruses the information that comes sequentially.

```
while (Serial.available())

    {

    char inChar=Serial.read();
```

In the wake of getting information sequentially we have put away it in a string and afterward hanging tight for Enter.

```
void serialEvent()

{

  while(Serial.available())

  {

    if(Serial.find("#A."))
```

```
{

    digitalWrite(led, HIGH);

    delay(1000);

    digitalWrite(led, LOW);

    while (Serial.available())

    {

    char inChar=Serial.read();

    str[i++]=inChar;

    if(inChar=='*')

    {

      temp=1;

      return;

    }
```

When Enter comes program begin to contrast got string and as of now characterized string and on the off chance that string coordinated, at that point a relative activity is performed by utilizing suitable direction that are given in code.

Code

```
#include<LiquidCrystal.h>
LiquidCrystal lcd(6,7,8,9,10,11);
#define Fan 3
#define Light 4
#define TV 5
int temp=0,i=0;
int led=13;
char str[15];
void setup()
{
 lcd.begin(16,2);
 Serial.begin(9600);
 pinMode(led, OUTPUT);
  pinMode(Fan, OUTPUT);
   pinMode(Light, OUTPUT);
    pinMode(TV, OUTPUT);


  lcd.setCursor(0,0);
 lcd.print("GSM Control Home");
 lcd.setCursor(0,1);
 lcd.print("  Automaton  ");
 delay(2000);
 lcd.clear();
 lcd.print("Hello world");
 delay(1000);
 lcd.setCursor(0,1);
```

```
lcd.print("System Ready");
Serial.println("AT+CNMI=2,2,0,0,0");
delay(500);
Serial.println("AT+CMGF=1");
delay(1000);
lcd.clear();
lcd.setCursor(0,0);
lcd.print("Fan  Light  TV ");
lcd.setCursor(0,1);
lcd.print("OFF   OFF  OFF ");
}
void loop()
{
 lcd.setCursor(0,0);
 lcd.print("Fan  Light  TV");
 if(temp==1)
 {
  check();
  temp=0;
  i=0;
  delay(1000);
 }
}
void serialEvent()
{
 while(Serial.available())
 {
  if(Serial.find("#A."))
  {
   digitalWrite(led, HIGH);
```

```
   delay(1000);
   digitalWrite(led, LOW);
   while (Serial.available())
   {
   char inChar=Serial.read();
   str[i++]=inChar;
   if(inChar=='*')
   {
    temp=1;
    return;
   }
   }
  }
 }
}
void check()
{
 if(!(strncmp(str,"tv on",5)))
 {
  digitalWrite(TV, HIGH);
  lcd.setCursor(13,1);
  lcd.print("ON ");
  delay(200);
 }


  else if(!(strncmp(str,"tv off",6)))
  {
  digitalWrite(TV, LOW);
  lcd.setCursor(13,1);
  lcd.print("OFF ");
```

```
  delay(200);
 }


  else if(!(strncmp(str,"fan on",5)))
 {
 digitalWrite(Fan, HIGH);
 lcd.setCursor(0,1);
 lcd.print("ON ");
 delay(200);
 }


  else if(!(strncmp(str,"fan off",7)))
 {
 digitalWrite(Fan, LOW);
 lcd.setCursor(0,1);
 lcd.print("OFF ");
 delay(200);
 }


  else if(!(strncmp(str,"light on",8)))
 {
 digitalWrite(Light, HIGH);
 lcd.setCursor(7,1);
 lcd.print("ON ");
 delay(200);
 }
```

```
  else if(!(strncmp(str,"light off",9)))
 {
  digitalWrite(Light, LOW);
  lcd.setCursor(7,1);
  lcd.print("OFF  ");
  delay(200);
 }


  else if(!(strncmp(str,"all on",6)))
 {
  digitalWrite(Light, HIGH);
  digitalWrite(Fan, HIGH);
  digitalWrite(TV, HIGH);
  lcd.setCursor(0,1);
  lcd.print("ON  ON  ON ");
  delay(200);
 }


  else if(!(strncmp(str,"all off",7)))
 {
  digitalWrite(Light, LOW);
  digitalWrite(Fan, LOW);
  digitalWrite(TV, LOW);
  lcd.setCursor(0,1);
  lcd.print("OFF OFF  OFF ");
  delay(200);
 }
}
```

8. PREPAID ENERGY METER UTILIZING GSM AND ARDUINO

Prepaid Electricity Energy Meter is a decent idea wherein you can energize its equalization, as we do in our cell phones. In this task we are making a robotized framework by utilizing Arduino and GSM module. You can revive the power balance through this framework, just by sending a SMS. It can likewise detach the home power supply association, if there is low or zero equalization in the framework. Also, this framework will peruses the vitality meter readings and naturally send a few updates to client's cell phone like low parity alert, cut off alarm, continue caution and revive alert.

Working explanation:

Here we have interfaced power vitality meter with Arduino utilizing the beat LED (Calibration or Cal) of power Energy meter. We just need to interface tis CAL LED to Arduino through an Optocoupler IC.

Components used:

- Arduino
- 16x2 LCD
- GSM Module
- Optocoupler 4n35
- Analogue Electricity Energy Meter
- POT
- Resistors
- Bulb and holder
- Connecting wires
- Power supply
- SIM card
- Mobile Phone

At the point when we catalyst the framework then it peruses past estimations of rupees put away in EEPROM and reestablishes them into the factors at that point checks the accessible parity with the pre-defined worth and make a move as per them, as in case accessible equalization is more noteworthy than 15 rupees, at that point Arduino turns On the power of home or office by utilizing transfer. Furthermore, on the off chance that equalization is under 15 rupees, at that point Arduino sends a SMS to client telephone with respect to low adjust alarm and mentioning to energize soon. Furthermore, on the off chance that equalization is under 5 rupees, at that point Arudino turns Off the power association of home and sends a SMS to client's telephone for 'Light Cut' alarm and mentioning to revive soon. GSM module has been utilized to send and get messages, you can check about GSM module and AT directions here.

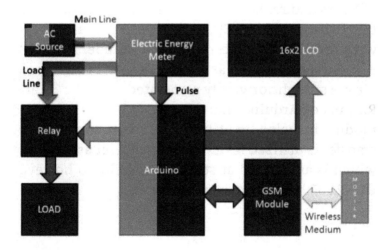

Presently when we have to revive our framework,

we can energize it basically by sending a SMS to the framework, through our Cellphone. Like in case we have to energize by 45 bucks, at that point we will send #45*, here # and * are prefix and postfix to the revive sum. Framework gets this message and concentrate revive sum and update the parity of framework. What's more, framework again turns On the power of the house or office.

Circuit Description:

Circuit associations for this Wireless Electricity Meter Reading Project, are appeared in the graph; we have utilized an Arduino UNO for handling every one of the things utilized in venture. A fluid precious stone presentation is utilized for showing the status of Units and remaining balance. Information pins of LCD to be specific RS, EN, D4, D5, D6, D7 are associated with Arduino computerized stick number 7, 6, 5, 4, 3, 2. Furthermore, Rx as well as Tx pins of GSM module are straightforwardly associated with the Tx and Rx pins of Arduino individually. What's more, GSM module is fueled by utilizing a 12 volt connector. A transfer is utilized for exchanging power association which is associated at stick 12 of Arduino however ULN2003 hand-off driver.

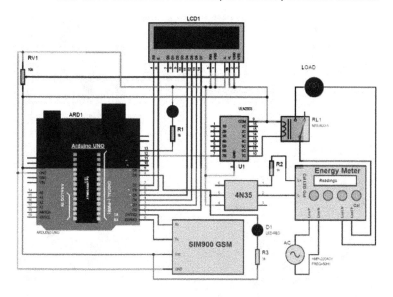

How to Connect Energy Meter with Arduino:

First client need to purchase an Analog Electricity Energy Meter. After it client needs to open it and discover the Pulse LED or Cal LED's terminals (cathode and Anode). Presently bind two wires at both the terminals and take it out from the vitality meter and afterward close vitality meter and tight the screws.

Presently client needs to interface anode terminal of LED at stick number 1 of Optocoupler and cathode terminal to stick 2. Stick number four of optocouper ought to be legitimately associated with ground. A LED and a Pull-up resistor are associated at stick number 5 of optocoupler. What's more, same terminal ought to go to the Arduino stick 8 as well.

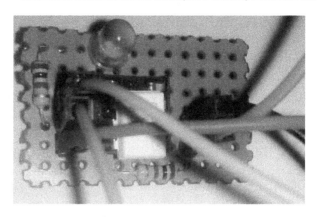

Calculation of Pulses and Units:

Prior to continuing for the figurings, first we have to remember the beat pace of vitality meter. There are two heartbeat paces of vitality meter initially is 1600 demon/kwh and second is 3200 pixie/kwh. So here we are utilizing 3200 devil/kwh heartbeat rate vitality meter.

So first we have to compute the Pulses for 100watt, implies how frequently Pulse LED will flicker in a moment, for the heap of 100 watts.

Pulse = (Pluse_rate*watt*time)/(1000*3600)

So beats for 100 watt bulb in 60 seconds, with vitality meter of 3200 demon/kwh heartbeat rate can be determined as beneath:

Pulses=3200*100*60/1000*3600

Heartbeats = ~5.33 beat every moment

Presently we have to figure Power factor of a solitary heartbeat, implies how much power will be expended in one heartbeat:

PF= watt/(hour*Pulse)

PF=100/60*5.33

PF=0.3125 watt in a solitary heartbeat

Units= PF*Total beat/1000

Absolute beats in an hour is around 5.33*60=320

Units = 0.3125*320/1000

Units = 0.1 every hour

On the off chance that a 100 watt bulb is lighting for a day, at that point it will expend

Units =0.1*24

Units = 2.4 Units

What's more, assume unit rate is at your locale is 5 rupees for each unit at that point

You need to pay for 2.4 Units Rs:

Rupees= 2.4*5 = 12 rupees

Programing explanation:

Above all else we incorporate required library and Define pins and factors that are required in our venture. This can be found in initial not many lines of our program code underneath.

After it we introduce the LCD, sequential correspondence, GSM and show some message.

After this in circle work we read sequential got information assuming any. Furthermore, peruses beat from vitality meter and show units and parity on LCD.

```
void setup()

{

lcd.begin(16,2);

Serial.begin(9600);

pinMode(led, OUTPUT);

.. ...

... .....
```

```
lcd.print("Hello world");

lcd.setCursor(0,1);

delay(2000);

lcd.print("GSM Initilizing...");

gsm_init();

.. ...

... ....
```

After this in circle work we read sequential got information assuming any. Furthermore, peruses beat from vitality meter and show units and equalization on LCD.

```
void loop()

{

  serialEvent();

  rupees=EEPROM.read(1);

  units=rupees/5.0;
```

```
lcd.setCursor(0,0);

lcd.print("Units:");

.. ...

... ....
```

void init_sms(),void send_data(String message), and void send_sms() capacities have been utilized to send SMS.

gsm_init() work is utilized for instating the GSM module for prepare to work with the framework. In this we initially sends AT direction to know whether GSM module is associated or not. After it we killed the reverberation and afterward check the system.

```
void gsm_init()

{

 lcd.clear();

 lcd.print("Finding Module..");

 boolean at_flag=1;

 while(at_flag)
```

```
.. ...

... ...
```

In check_status() work framework understands association and Balance conditions; like whether power equalization is more prominent than as far as possible. In case parity is under 15 ,, at that point it alarms the client by sending the SMS caution of 'Low Balance' and in the event that parity is under 5 rupees, at that point framework will cut the power and advise the client by sending SMS utilizing GSM module.

```
void check_status()

{

  if(rupees>15)

  {

    digitalWrite(relay, HIGH);

    flag1 =0;

    .. ...

    ... ....
```

send_confirmaiton_sms() work is utilized for sending affirmation message to the client if revive has been done and it likewise update the parity in the framework.

decode_message() work is utilized for unraveling the sum figure from the SMS message, by utilizing the # and * as beginning and closure character.

read_pulse() work is utilized for perusing beat from the Energy meter through optocoupler IC. What's more, update the unit and parity.

```
void read_pulse()

{

  if(!digitalRead(pulsein))

  {

   digitalWrite(led, HIGH);

   if(units<1){}

   .. ...

   ... ....
```

serialEvent() work is utilized for sequential correspondence and getting the message.

Code

```
#include<EEPROM.h>
#include <LiquidCrystal.h>
LiquidCrystal lcd(7,6,5,4,3,2);
int led=13;
#define pulsein 8
#define relay 12
unsigned int pusle_count=0;
float units=0;
unsigned int rupees=0;
 float watt_factor=0.3125;
unsigned int temp=0,i=0,x=0,k=0;
char str[70],flag1=0,flag2=0;
String bal="";
void setup()
{
 lcd.begin(16,2);
 Serial.begin(9600);
 pinMode(led, OUTPUT);
 pinMode(pulsein, INPUT);
 pinMode(relay, OUTPUT);
 digitalWrite(pulsein, HIGH);
 lcd.setCursor(0,0);
 lcd.print("Automatic Energy");
 lcd.setCursor(0,1);
 lcd.print("   Meter   ");
 delay(2000);
```

```
lcd.clear();
lcd.print("Hello world");
delay(2000);
lcd.clear();
lcd.print("GSM Initilizing...");
gsm_init();
lcd.clear();
lcd.print("System Ready");
Serial.println("AT+CNMI=2,2,0,0,0");
init_sms();
send_data("System Ready");
send_sms();
delay(1000);
digitalWrite(led, LOW);
lcd.clear();
// EEPROM.write(1,0);
// rupees=EEPROM.read(1);
}
void loop()
{
  serialEvent();
  rupees=EEPROM.read(1);
  units=rupees/5.0;
  lcd.setCursor(0,0);
  lcd.print("Units:");
  lcd.print(units);
  lcd.print("   ");
  lcd.setCursor(0,1);
  if(rupees<15)
  lcd.print("LOW Balance:");
```

```
  else
  lcd.print("Balance:");
  lcd.print(rupees);
  lcd.print("   ");
  read_pulse();
  check_status();
  if(temp==1)
  {
   decode_message();
   send_confirmation_sms();
  }
}
void serialEvent()
{
 while(Serial.available())
 {
  char ch=(char)Serial.read();
  str[i++]=ch;
  if(ch == '*')
  {
   temp=1;
   lcd.clear();
   lcd.print("Message Received");
   delay(500);
   break;
  }
 }
}
void init_sms()
{
```

```
 Serial.println("AT+CMGF=1");
 delay(200);
 Serial.println("AT+CMGS=\"+918287114222\"");
 delay(200);
}
void send_data(String message)
{
 Serial.println(message);
 delay(200);
}
void send_sms()
{
 Serial.write(26);
}
void read_pulse()
{
  if(!digitalRead(pulsein))
  {
   digitalWrite(led, HIGH);
   //count++;
   //units=watt_factor*count/1000;
   if(units<1){}
   else
   units--;
   rupees=units*5;
   EEPROM.write(1,rupees);
   while(!digitalRead(pulsein));
   digitalWrite(led,LOW);
   // delay(2000);
  }
```

```
}
void check_status()
{
  if(rupees>15)
  {
   digitalWrite(relay, HIGH);
   flag1=0;
   flag2=0;
  }
  if(rupees<15 && flag1==0)
  {
  lcd.setCursor(0,1);
  lcd.print("LOW Balance    ");
  init_sms();
  send_data("Energy Meter Balance Alert:");
  send_data("Low Balance\n");
  Serial.println(rupees);
  delay(200);
     send_data("Please recharge your energy meter
soon.\n Thank you");
  send_sms();
  message_sent();
  flag1=1;
  }
  if(rupees<5 && flag2==0)
  {
  digitalWrite(relay, LOW);
  lcd.clear();
  lcd.print("Light Cut Due to");
  lcd.setCursor(0,1);
```

```
    lcd.print("Low Balance");
    delay(2000);
    lcd.clear();
    lcd.print("Please Recharge ");
    lcd.setCursor(0,1);
    lcd.print("UR Energy Meter ");
    init_sms();
        send_data("Energy Meter Balance Alert:\nLight
cut due to low Balance\nPlease recharge your energy
meter soon.\n Thank you");
    send_sms();
    message_sent();
    flag2=1;
  }
}
void decode_message()
{
 x=0,k=0,temp=0;
  while(x<i)
  {
  while(str[x]=='#')
  {
   x++;
   bal="";
   while(str[x]!='*')
   {
    bal+=str[x++];
   }
  }
  x++;
```

```
  }
  bal+='\0';
}
void send_confirmation_sms()
{
  int recharge_amount=bal.toInt();
  rupees+=recharge_amount;
  EEPROM.write(1,rupees);
  lcd.clear();
  lcd.print("Energy Meter ");
  lcd.setCursor(0,1);
  lcd.print("Recharged:");
  lcd.print(recharge_amount);
  init_sms();
   send_data("Energy Meter Balance Alert:\nYour en-
ergy meter has been recharged Rs:");
  send_data(bal);
  send_data("Total Balance:");
  Serial.println(rupees);
  delay(200);
       send_data("Eelctricity Has Been Connected
\nThank you");
  send_sms();
  temp=0;
  i=0;
  x=0;
  k=0;
  delay(1000);
  message_sent();
}
```

```
void message_sent()
{
 lcd.clear();
 lcd.print("Message Sent.");
 delay(1000);
}
void gsm_init()
{
 lcd.clear();
 lcd.print("Finding Module..");
 boolean at_flag=1;
 while(at_flag)
 {
  Serial.println("AT");
  while(Serial.available()>0)
  {
   if(Serial.find("OK"))
   at_flag=0;
  }
  delay(1000);
 }
 lcd.clear();
 lcd.print("Module Connected..");
 delay(1000);
 lcd.clear();
 lcd.print("Disabling ECHO");
 boolean echo_flag=1;
 while(echo_flag)
 {
  Serial.println("ATE0");
```

```
  while(Serial.available()>0)
  {
   if(Serial.find("OK"))
   echo_flag=0;
  }
  delay(1000);
 }
 lcd.clear();
 lcd.print("Echo OFF");
 delay(1000);
 lcd.clear();
 lcd.print("Finding Network..");
 boolean net_flag=1;
 while(net_flag)
 {
  Serial.println("AT+CPIN?");
  while(Serial.available()>0)
  {
   if(Serial.find("+CPIN: READY"))
   net_flag=0;
  }
  delay(1000);
 }
 lcd.clear();
 lcd.print("Network Found..");
 delay(1000);
 lcd.clear();
}
```

9. APPLAUD SWITCH UTILIZING ARDUINO

In this undertaking we are gonna to make Clapper circuit utilizing the idea of ADC (Analog to Digital Conversion) in ARDUINO UNO. We are gonna to utilize a MIC and Uno to detect the sound and trigger a reaction. This Clap ON Clap OFF switch fundamentally kills ON or the gadget, by utilizing the applaud sound, as switch. We have recently assembled Clap switch and Clap ON Clap OFF switch, utilizing 555 Timer IC.

On applauding there will be a pinnacle signal at the MIC which is a lot higher than typical, this sign is nourished to the speaker, however a High Pass Filter. This enhanced voltage sign is bolstered to ADC, which changes over this high voltage into a number. So there will be a top in the ADC perusing of the UNO. On this pinnacle identification we will flip a LED on the board, on each applaud. This venture has been clarified in detail underneath.

MIC or Microphone is a sound detecting transducer, which essentially changes over sound vitality into electrical vitality, so with this sensor we have sound as evolving voltage. We normally record or sense sound through this gadget. This transducer is utilized in every single cell phone and PCs. A normal MIC resembles,

Deciding the extremity of Condenser Mic:

MIC has two terminals one is certain and another is negative. Mic extremity can be discovered utilizing a Multi-Meter. Take the positive test of Multi-Meter (put the meter in DIODE TESTING mode) as well as associate it to one terminal of MIC as well as the -ve test to the next terminal of MIC. On the off chance that you get the readings on the screen, at that point the terminal of +ve (MIC) is at -ve terminal of Multi-Meter. Or in case you can just discover the terminals by taking a gander at it, the negative terminal has a few welding lines, associated with the metal instance of the mic. This availability, from negative terminal to its metal case can likewise be tried utilizing progression analyzer, to discover the negative terminal.

Components Required:

Hardware:

ARDUINO UNO, a condenser mic (explained above), power supply (5v)

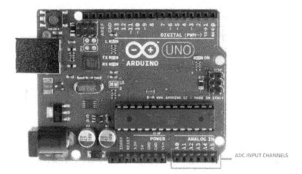

2N3904 NPN transistor,

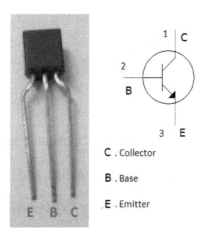

C . Collector

B . Base

E . Emitter

100nF capacitors (2 pieces), one 100uF capacitor,

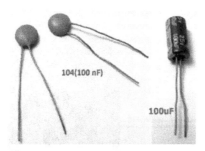

1K O resistor, 1M? resistor, 15K? resistor (2 pieces), one LED,

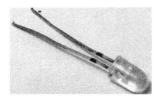

What's more, Breadboard and Connecting wires.

Programming: Arduino IDE - Arduino daily.

Circuit Diagram and Working Explanation:

The circuit outline of the clapper circuit is appeared in underneath figure:

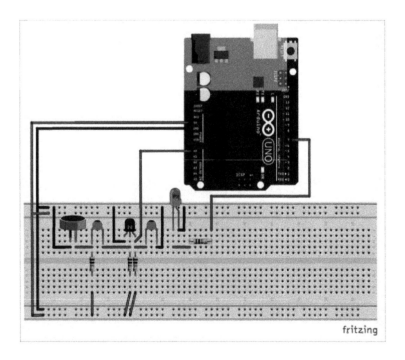

We have isolated the working into four sections, that is: Filtration, Amplification, Analog-computerized change and programming to flip the LED

At whatever point there is sound, the MIC lifts it up and changes over it into voltage, direct to the greatness of sound. So for a higher sound we have higher worth and for lower sound we have lower esteem. This worth is first encouraged to the High Pass Filter for filtration. At that point this sifted worth is bolstered to the transistor for enhancement and transistor gives the intensified yield at the authority. This gatherer sign is encouraged to the ADC0 channel of the UNO, for Analog to Digital change. Furthermore, finally Arduino is modified to flip the LED, associated at PIN 7 of PORTD, each time ADC channel A0 goes past a specific level.

1. Filtration:

As a matter of first importance we will speak quickly about R-C High Pass Filter, which has been utilized to sift through the commotions. It's anything but difficult to structure and comprises of a solitary resistor and single capacitor. For this circuit we needn't bother with a lot of detail, so we will keep it basic. A high pass channel permits sign of high recurrence go from contribution to yield, as it were the information sign shows up at the yield if the recurrence of sign is higher than the channel recommended recurrence. For the present, we need not to stress over these qualities in light of the fact that here we are not structuring a sound intensifier. A high pass channel is appeared in the circuit.

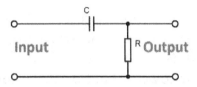

After this channel, voltage sign is sustained to the transistor for enhancement.

2. Intensification:

The voltage of MIC is low and can't be nourished to UNO for ADC (Analog to Digital Conversion), so for this we structure a basic enhancer utilizing a transistor. Here we have planned a solitary transistor speaker for enhancing the MIC voltages. This intensified voltage sign is additionally bolstered to the ADC0 channel of Arduino.

3. Simple to Digital Conversion:

ARDUINO has 6 ADC channels. Among those, any one or every one of them can be utilized as contributions for simple voltage. The UNO ADC is of 10 piece goals (so the whole number qualities from (0-(2^{10}) 1023)).This implies that it will guide input voltages somewhere in the range of 0 and 5 volts into whole number qualities somewhere in the range of 0 and 1023. So for each (5/1024= 4.9mV) per unit.

Presently, for the UNO to change over simple sign into advanced sign, we have to Use ADC Channel of ARDUINO UNO, with the assistance of beneath capacities:

1. analogRead(pin);

2. analogReference();

UNO ADC channels have a default reference estimation of 5V. This implies we can give a most extreme info voltage of 5V for ADC transformation at any information channel. Since certain sensors give voltages from 0-2.5V, so with a 5V reference, we get lesser exactness, so we have a guidance that empowers us to change this reference esteem. So for changing the reference esteem we have "analogReference();"

In our circuit, we have left this reference voltage to the default, so we can peruse an incentive from ADC channel 0, by straightforwardly calling capacity "analogRead(pin);", here "stick" speaks to stick where we associated the simple sign, for this situation it would be "A0". The incentive from ADC can be taken into a whole number as "int sensorValue = analogRead(A0); ", by this guidance the incentive from ADC gets put away in the number "sensorValue". Presently, we have the transistor esteem in computerized structure, in the memory of UNO.

4. Program Arduino to Toggle the LED on each Clap:

Under typical occurrences, the MIC gives ordinary flag thus we have ordinary advanced esteems in the UNO, however on applauding there a pinnacle gave by the MIC, with this we have a pinnacle computerized an incentive in the UNO, we can program the UNO to flip a LED ON and OFF at whatever point there is a pinnacle. So on first applaud the LED turns ON and remains ON. On second applaud the LED turns OFF and remains OFF until the following applaud. With this we have the clapper circuit. Check the program Code underneath.

Code

```
const int analogInPin = A0; // Analog input pin 0
int sensorValue = 0;
void setup()
{
DDRD = 0xFF;
}
void loop()
{
sensorValue = analogRead(analogInPin);   //read ADC value on channel 0
if(sensorValue>60)
{
  PORTD ^=(1<<7); //If there is a peak toggle the LED on and OFF on pin7.
```

```
delay(250);
 }
}
```

◆ ◆ ◆

10. REMOTE NOTICE BOARD UTILIZING GSM AND ARDUINO

Remote notice board is very specific term for this venture, as it has a very wide degree as opposed to simply being a basic notice board. First we ought to comprehend the motivation behind this undertaking, in this framework we can show a message or notice to some show gadget like LCD, and this message can be effectively set or changed from wherever on the planet, just by utilizing the SMS office of your portable handset. Whatever notice we need to show, simply send the SMS of that content, with some prefix and postfix.

This is exceptionally valuable in Hotels, Malls, school, workplaces and can be utilized anyplace, even at home. Like you can set the message like "Don't upset" at your lodging's entryway, can set message at your home's entryway step when you are away, and obviously it is utilized as notice board in schools, universities, film lobbies and so on. Also, indeed, it's simply not a basic Message board, the convenience of this task is that you can set or change the message or notice from anyplace, simply sending SMS from your telephone.

We have recently utilized the SMS office of cell phone for home security and control the home devices remotely: PIR Sensor and GSM Based Security System and Global System for Mobile Based Home Automation utilizing Arduino

Working Explanation:

In this venture, Arduino UNO is utilized for controlling the entire procedure, GSM module (SIM900A) to get the SMS/message sent from cell phone and LCD to show the message.

We can send some message or notice like "#Hello world*", "#We Welcomes You*" through the SMS. Here we have utilized a prefix in the message string that is '#'. This prefix is utilized to recognize the beginning of the message or notice. Furthermore, '*' is utilized as postfix to demonstrate the finish of the message or notice.

At the point when we send SMS from cell phone to GSM module then GSM gets that SMS as well as sends it to Arduino. Presently Arduino read this SMS and concentrate principle notice message from the got string and stores in another string. And afterward sends the extricated message to 16x2 LCD by utilizing suitable directions.

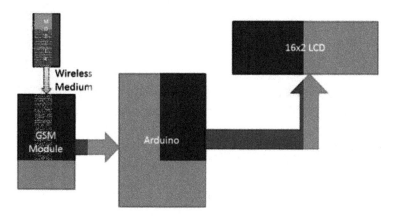

Further working of this framework is clarified in the 'Code Description' segment beneath. Before we dive into programming subtleties we should think about GSM module.

GSM Module:

GSM module is utilized in numerous specialized gadgets which depend on GSM (Global System for Mobile Communications) innovation. It is utilized to connect with GSM system utilizing a PC. GSM module just comprehends AT directions, and can react in like manner. The most essential order is "AT", on the off chance that GSM react OK, at that point it is working great else it react with "Mistake". There are different AT directions like ATA for answer a call, ATD to dial a call, AT+CMGR to peruse the message, AT+CMGS to send the sms and so on. AT directions ought to be trailed via Carriage return for example \r (0D in hex), like "AT+CMGS\r". We can utilize GSM module utilizing these directions:

ATE0 For reverberation off

AT+CNMI=2,2,0,0,0 <ENTER> Auto opened message Receiving. (No compelling reason to open message)

ATD<Mobile Number>; <ENTER> making a call (ATD +919610126059;\r\n)

AT+CMGF=1 <ENTER> Selecting Text mode

AT+CMGS="Mobile Number" <ENTER> Assigning beneficiary's portable number

>>Now we can compose our message

>>After composing message

Ctrl+Z send message order (26 in decimal).

ENTER=0x0d in HEX

The SIM900 is a finished Quad-band Global System for Mobile/General Packet Radio Service Module which conveys GSM/GPRS 850/900/1800/1900MHz execution for voice, SMS as well as Data with low power utilization.

Circuit Description:

Associations of Wireless Notice Board utilizing GSM and Arduino are straightforward and appeared in the figure beneath. Here a fluid precious stone presentation (LCD) is utilized for show the "Notice" or message, which is sent however the cell phone as SMS. Information pins of LCD to be specific RS, EN, D4, D5, D6, D7 are associated with arduino advanced stick number 7, 6, 5, 4, 3, 2. What's more, Rx and Tx stick of GSM module is legitimately associated at Tx and Rx stick of Arduino separately. What's more, GSM module is fueled by utilizing a 12 volt connector.

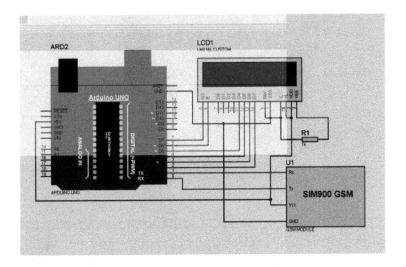

Code Description:

The code of the program is effectively justifiable; the new thing here is GSN instatement work gsm_init(), which is clarified at last.

In the program, most importantly we incorporate library for fluid precious stone presentation (LCD) and afterward we characterizes information and control pins for LCD and a few factors.

```
#include <LiquidCrystal.h>
```

```
LiquidCrystal lcd(7,6,5,4,3,2);

int led=13;

int temp=0,i=0,x=0,k=0;

char str[100],msg[32];
```

After this, sequential correspondence is introduced at 9600 bps and provides guidance to utilized stick. Furthermore, introduce GSM Module in arrangement circle.

```
void setup()

{

  lcd.begin(16,2);

  Serial.begin(9600);

  pinMode(led, OUTPUT);

  digitalWrite(led, HIGH);

  lcd.print("GSM Initilizing...");

  gsm_init();
```

```
lcd.setCursor(0,0);

lcd.print("Wireless Notice");
```

For accepting information sequentially we utilize two capacities, one is Serial.available which checks any sequential information is coming or not and other one is Serial.read which peruses the information that comes sequentially.

```
void serialEvent()

{

  while(Serial.available())

  {

    char ch=(char)Serial.read();

    str[i++]=ch;

    if(ch == '*')

    {

      temp=1;

      lcd.clear();
```

```
    lcd.print("Message Received");

    delay(1000);

  }

 }

}
```

In the wake of accepting information sequentially, we store it in a string and this string is checked for '#' and '*', to locate the beginning and closure of the Notice or message. At that point at last Notice is imprinted on LCD utilizing lcd.print:

```
void loop()

{

  for(unsigned int t=0;t<60000;t++)

  {

    serialEvent();

  if(temp==1)

  {
```

```
x=0,k=0,temp=0;

while(x<i)

{

  while(str[x]=='#')

  {

    x++;

    while(str[x]!='*')

    {

      msg[k++]=str[x++];
```

Instatement work 'gsm_init()' for GSM is significant here, where right off the bat, GSM module is checked whether it is associated or not by sending 'AT' direction to GSM module. In case reaction OK is gotten, implies it is prepared. Framework continues checking for the module until it gets prepared or until 'alright' is gotten. At that point ECHO is killed by sending the ATE0 order, generally GSM module will resound every one of the directions. At that point at last Network accessibility is checked through the 'AT+CPIN?' direction, whenever embedded card is SIM card and PIN is available, it gives the reaction +CPIN: READY.

This is likewise check more than once until the system is found.

```
void gsm_init()

{

  lcd.clear();

  lcd.print("Finding Module..");

  boolean at_flag=1;

  while(at_flag)

  {

    Serial.println("AT");

    while(Serial.available()>0)

    {

      if(Serial.find("OK"))

      at_flag=0;

    }
```

```
  delay(1000);

 }
```

Code

```
#include <LiquidCrystal.h>
LiquidCrystal lcd(7,6,5,4,3,2);
int led=13;
int temp=0,i=0,x=0,k=0;
char str[100],msg[32];
void setup()
{
 lcd.begin(16,2);
 Serial.begin(9600);
 pinMode(led, OUTPUT);
 digitalWrite(led, HIGH);
 lcd.print("GSM Initilizing...");
 gsm_init();
 lcd.setCursor(0,0);
 lcd.print("Wireless Notice");
 lcd.setCursor(0,1);
 lcd.print("  Board   ");
 delay(2000);
 lcd.clear();
 lcd.print("Hello world");
 delay(1000);
 lcd.setCursor(0,1);
 lcd.print("System Ready");
 Serial.println("AT+CNMI=2,2,0,0,0");
 delay(500);
```

```
 Serial.println("AT+CMGF=1");
 delay(1000);
 digitalWrite(led, LOW);
}
void loop()
{
 for(unsigned int t=0;t<60000;t++)
 {
  serialEvent();
 if(temp==1)
 {
  x=0,k=0,temp=0;
  while(x<i)
  {
   while(str[x]=='#')
   {
    x++;
    while(str[x]!='*')
    {
     msg[k++]=str[x++];
    }
   }
   x++;
  }
  msg[k]='\0';
  lcd.clear();
  lcd.print(msg);
  delay(1000);
  temp=0;
  i=0;
```

```
  x=0;
  k=0;
 }
 }
 lcd.scrollDisplayLeft();
}
void serialEvent()
{
 while(Serial.available())
 {
  char ch=(char)Serial.read();
  str[i++]=ch;
  if(ch == '*')
  {
   temp=1;
   lcd.clear();
   lcd.print("Message Received");
   delay(1000);
  }
 }
}
void gsm_init()
{
 lcd.clear();
 lcd.print("Finding Module..");
 boolean at_flag=1;
 while(at_flag)
 {
  Serial.println("AT");
  while(Serial.available()>0)
```

```
{
 if(Serial.find("OK"))
 at_flag=0;
}
 delay(1000);
}
lcd.clear();
lcd.print("Module Connected..");
delay(1000);
lcd.clear();
lcd.print("Disabling ECHO");
boolean echo_flag=1;
while(echo_flag)
{
 Serial.println("ATE0");
 while(Serial.available()>0)
 {
  if(Serial.find("OK"))
  echo_flag=0;
 }
 delay(1000);
}
lcd.clear();
lcd.print("Echo OFF");
delay(1000);
lcd.clear();
lcd.print("Finding Network..");
boolean net_flag=1;
while(net_flag)
{
```

```
  Serial.println("AT+CPIN?");
  while(Serial.available()>0)
  {
   if(Serial.find("+CPIN: READY"))
   net_flag=0;
  }
  delay(1000);
 }
 lcd.clear();
 lcd.print("Network Found..");
 delay(1000);
 lcd.clear();
}
```

THANK YOU !!!

♦ ♦ ♦

www.ingramcontent.com/pod-product-compliance
Lightning Source LLC
Chambersburg PA
CBHW071131050326
40690CB00008B/1429